Giulio Romano

Giulio Romano

Arnoldo Mondadori Arte

Texts by Franco Ambrosio
Translation by Richard Sadleir

© 1991 by **Arnoldo Mondadori Arte,** Milan
Elemond Editori Associati

Table of Contents

Giulio Romano

"It's often said that Giulio Romano was the pupil of Raphael; but one might just as truly say that he was the pupil of his century." These words by Goethe give a good idea of the scope of the work of Giulio Romano, who was trained in the biggest and most modern artist's workshop in Italy—that of Raphael—but soon came to dominate his age, creating a model of style and taste for the most refined courts of Europe in the period of Mannerism.

Raphael's personality and his standing as an artist did, however, leave evident traces in his work, and these appear in three ways. Firstly, his artistic versatility, the ability to express his creativity in a wide range of ways: his work consistently centred on draughtsmanship but also expanded into painting, architecture, goldsmith's work, the designing of festivities, triumphs, and both permanent and ephemeral structures. Secondly, Raphael's legacy appears in Giulio's profoundly sensuous joy in colour, though the techniques and meanings expressed by the two artists differ widely. Finally, Giulio repeated Raphael's domination of the artistic and cultural life of the Rome of the popes in Mantua, at the court of Federico Gonzaga, where—partly from choice though mainly by necessity—he took on many new tasks.

The move to Mantua was not the result of chance or need, but of pressing invitations from the Gonzagas. Almost two decades earlier the city had been deprived of Mantegna, who had introduced his erudite and classicizing art to the city, and this precedent, strengthened by the "insatiable passion... for ancient things" of Isabella d'Este, Federico's mother, led to the summons of this disciple of the classical Raphael who had already made a name by his learning and pagan subjects.

In Mantua, Giulio soon revealed a very different kind of secular style from Mantegna's, and the softness of his handling (Raphaelesque in origin), contrasted with the "drier" manner of his predecessor. His influence soon made itself felt. From the third decade of the sixteenth century, Giulio Romano's hand was present in all the state's architectural and artistic undertakings, with a personal imprint that eclipsed everything that had gone before and became a cultural landmark in northern Italy.

Titian, Portrait of Giulio Romano,
c. 1536. Private Collection.

Apprenticeship in Raphael's Workshop and the Roman Period

The date of Giulio Romano's birth is uncertain. The records available are the funeral oration delivered in Mantua on his death, which gives 1499 as the date of birth, and Giorgio Vasari's biographical work, *Le Vite de' più eccellenti pittori, scultori e architettori* (1568), which gives 1492. These records are not very reliable, because—apart from the seven-year difference between the dates, the two texts are highly inaccurate in other ways. However, he was definitely born in Rome, and his father was the "*nobilis vir*" Pietro Pippi "de Ianutiis" (i.e. de' Giannuzzi).

Giulio began his apprenticeship in about 1515, as a worker in Raphael's *bottega* in Rome. As a young helper he worked on the cycles of paintings executed by Raphael in the Stanze and the Loggias of the Vatican (Plates 4-8), in the Loggia di Psiche at the Farnesina Palace (Plates 1-3), and his hand is now also identified in various canvases from Raphael's last period, such as the *Virgin and Child with the Infant Saint John* (Louvre, Paris), and the *Spinola Madonna* and *Novar Madonna* (National Gallery of Scotland, Edinburgh).

Apart from their collaboration, Giulio's relationship with Raphael was one of deep affection and the strength of this attachment was largely due to Giulio's character: Vasari describes him in the *Lives* as "strong, proud, confident, capricious, many-sided, abundant, and universal," and adds that he was "very sweet of speech, jovial, affable, charming and possessed of excellent manners, which were the reason that he was so beloved by Raphael, who could not have loved him more if he had been his son; so that it came about that Raphael always employed him in his works of greatest importance."

Giulio's first independent work was the *Portrait of Joanna of Aragon* (Louvre, Paris; Plate 9), which shows signs of his departure from Raphael's manner. Despite an attempt to imitate Raphael's artistic vision and win his approval, Giulio here introduced what was to become one of the outstanding features of his work, the break between the person portrayed and the setting. He deliberately rejected the harmony so carefully sought after by Raphael between the figure and the surrounding space, not subordinating the latter to the former, but instead constructing both as different episodes in a wider perspective.

On 6 April 1520, Raphael died. His workshop, together with the unfinished works, passed to Giulio Romano and Gianfrancesco Penni, the pair being linked closely by five years together in Raphael's workshop.

The four years that followed were fertile and eventful ones for their work as artists. The partnership with Penni was strengthened; together they continued the paintings in the Sala di Costantino in the Vatican, commissioned by Leo X, and signed a contract for the completion of the *Coronation of the Virgin* for the nuns of Monteluce (Pinacoteca Vaticana, Rome; Plate 10). As "Raphael's assistant," Giulio was invited for the first time to Mantua by Federico Gonzaga. Meanwhile, he was gradually making his name as an independent artist, mainly through works like the *Christ in Glory with Four Saints* (*Deesis*) (Pinacoteca Nazionale, Parma; Plates 11, 12), the *Madonna Hertz* (Palazzo Barberini, Rome; Plate 16); the *Sacra Conversazione Fugger* (Santa Maria dell'Anima, Rome; Plates 13, 14), and the drawings for the series of *Modi*, so called because its theme is the different positions of sixteen couples making love. These works are all very difficult to date exactly but they belong to this period.

Giulio's family life was deeply troubled. The marriage of his sister Gerolama to the Florentine Lorenzetto (Lorenzo di Ludovico, sculptor and architect) in 1523 was followed within the same year by the deaths of his brothers Domenico and Francesco and his sisters Laura and Silvia. His finances also seem to have been shaky, despite his paternal inheritance, for Gerolama's dowry consisted almost wholly of the payment for the *Transfiguration* (Pinacoteca Vaticana, Rome), originally commissioned from Raphael by the Cardinal Giulio de' Medici and for which Giulio received payment through the good offices of Baldassarre Castiglione.

It was also Castiglione that insisted on Giulio's acceptance of the invitation to move to the Gonzaga court in Mantua, and he accompanied him on the journey, which began on 6 October 1521 and ended sixteen days later.

Works in Mantua. The Palazzo Te

When he arrived in Mantua, Giulio Romano could already boast of a number of architectural designs for villas and palaces in Rome, but his fame was mainly based on his paintings, and Federico Gonzaga, whose express intention was to employ him in both fields, revealed his personal conviction by addressing him as "Iulio Pictor."

However Giulio's first two years in Mantua were devoted mainly to architecture, as appears from his appointment as "supervisor of roads" and "director of buildings" to the Gonzagas (20 November 1526), and above all from the start of construction of the Palazzo Te, probably towards the end of 1525. Within a few months, however, he was also put in charge of painting, and his responsibilities increased in importance until he finally became the organizer of the pageant of life at court, the same role that Raphael had played for Leo X.

The quality that enabled him to rise so high and so rapidly was his astonishing fertility in supplying designs for silverwork, furnishings, frescoes, paintings, palaces, villas and for gardens, all stamped with his own taste.

Palazzo Te is an epitome, the highest expression of Giulio Romano's achievements at the court of the Gonzagas. The singularity of the work begins with its name "Te," derived from a mediaeval term "Teieto" used for the broad grassy area outside Mantua's mediaeval walls. There, amid green pastures, stood the walls of the ancient stables of the Gonzagas, which gave the *marchese* Federico the idea for a villa and a garden "designed" by the waters of the many small lakes surrounding the town.

Vasari tells us there were two phases in the construction work. The first was bounded by the northern part of the pre-existing boundary wall—"a little place where one might go to and sometimes have lunch or dinner outdoors"—followed by a second phase in which "the whole building was turned into a great palace." The earliest records referring to the new building are dated February 1526 (though work must have started some months before) and refer to the quantities of paint brushes, plaster, marble for doors and fireplaces, and ancient statues, purchased for decoration. The care taken in laying in these materials shows that the décor was considered the most important part of the whole work. It was built quickly, if one takes into account the interruption of work between 1529

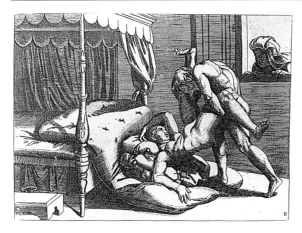

Marcantonio Raimondi, after Giulio Romano, engraving of the series of Modi. *Albertina, Vienna.*

Marcantonio Raimondi, after Giulio Romano, engraving of the series of the Modi. *Bibliothèque Nationale, Paris.*

and 1531 to restructure the Palazzo Ducale, and it is probable that Giulio had laid down a precise schedule of work and all the drawings were completed before building began. We know the names of about ten collaborators on the paintings and carvings. Their task was to complete the scenes after Giulio had prepared them and given the first touches to serve as a guide.

Stylistic analysis suggests that the first chamber to be completed was the Sala dei Cavalli, with all the assistants sharing in the work (Plates 19,20). This chamber is devoted to the exaltation of the horse, one of Federico Gonzaga's great passions, while the *Stories of Hercules*, placed above the horses, also refers to the Duke and his warlike qualities. The first phase also included the decoration of the adjoining Sala di Psiche (Plates 21-25), which was to serve as a model for generations of Mannerist painters. This chamber, with its sumptuous, sensual representations and bold foreshortening, illustrates the adventures of Psyche, persecuted by Venus and finally triumphant in his marriage to Cupid and the achievement of immortality, a story which is based on the *Metamorphoses* of Apuleius. Apart from the openly erotic and pagan subjects, the decoration as a whole may be interpreted as symbolizing the spirit's liberation from earthly attachments for a mystical purpose.

Religious implications are also present in the Sala dei Giganti (Plates 26, 31), on the same side of the palace and open to the south, one of the most spectacular examples of Renaissance grotesque. The scenes, based on the *Gigantomachia* of Ovid, depict the Giants' attack against Olympus and the punishment meted out by Jove, in a hail of stones and boulders, allegorically alluding to God's defeat of the rebel angels and their fall.

The steps in the completion of the Palazzo Te are not documented sufficiently clearly to allow us to reconstruct them fully, but it is known that the work was ended by the middle of 1534. This does not imply that work went ahead slowly, because Giulio Romano and his helpers—urged on by Federico Gonzaga, who at times even threatened them with bodily punishment—worked with even greater celerity than Raphael. But the rooms to be decorated numbered more than twenty, and the work required a high degree of organization to coordinate the financing, the designs, the work of masons, sculptors, painters, plasterers, carpenters and gilders.

The final result was a sumptuous villa, constructed on a country estate laid out on two islands. The smaller contained "the palace, with chambers, loggias, and staterooms, and a garden and the home of the gardener," while the larger contained the pastures with outhouses, stables, haylofts, dovecotes, the homes of the farmers and the stableboys.

At present the Palazzo Te corresponds only partially to the complex conceived by Giulio Romano; over the last three centuries there have been numerous alterations, starting with that ordered by the Austrian administration at the end of the eighteenth century, when the Accademia delle Belle Arti in Mantua was entrusted with the restoration of the villa, which had been seriously damaged during the attacks on the city.

At the beginning of the twentieth century, with the demolition of the city walls and the filling in of the canal bounding the island of Te, the palace became integrated into the outskirts of Mantua. In this way the setting that had been linked in so singular a manner to the city and the countryside was lost.

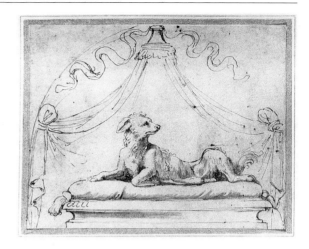

Drawing for a monument to a dog, c. 1526. Cooper-Hewitt Museum of Design, New-York.

Drawing for casket with the eagle of the Gonzagas, after 1525. Metropolitan Museum of Art, New York.

Mantua and Environs (1526-1546)

During the nine years of building the Palazzo Te, Giulio Romano was also busy producing his many-sided, exuberant works. This later led Cardinal Ercole Gonzaga, Federico's successor in the dukedom, to confess that "Giulio was more master of the state than he was"; but this hectic rate of work was the immediate result of the urgent demands of Federico Gonzaga. These requests included a commission for a marble monument for a pet dog (1526) and the order to repair the house of a Captain of Arms (1527). Tasks of this kind were the exception, but they give some idea of the immense range of tasks on which Giulio was employed. For the same reason it is worth mentioning the death-mask of Giovanni dalle Bande Nere (1526) and the design for a monument to commemorate Piero Strozzi.

Also belonging to this first phase of Giulio's work in Mantua was the scenery designed for Charles V's visit to Mantua in March 1530. It included a bridge of boats across the Po at Saviola, and a column erected in the cathedral square, that was "very tall [35 metres] and beautiful, with beautiful verses and inscriptions, with a figure of victory holding a laurel branch on top."

Giulio had been granted Mantuan citizenship in 1526 and in the midst of this unflagging output, three years later he married Elena, the daughter of Francesco Guazzi, and lived with her in a house in the district of the Unicorno, his home for the rest of his life. This was also the moment when the growth of his prestige began to win him concrete rewards from the *marchese* Federico: the use of a building on the bridge of the Mulini, and generous payments that enabled him to purchase a second house and an estate at Bellaguarda di Borgoforte.

On 8 April 1530, Federico Gonzaga became duke and the following year, for his marriage to Margherita Paleologa, he commissioned Giulio to enlarge the castle of Mantua, the Gonzaga's official residence and the administrative centre of the state. The original plan was expanded by the construction of the Palazzina di Margherita Paleologa (demolished in 1899), a kind of small villa-annex to the ducal suite. The work was complete (save for some frescoed interiors put off until the weather was more favourable) by 16 November 1531, the day when the bride and groom made their official entry to Mantua.

Giulio's outstanding achievements in the castle of Mantua probably led Ercole II d'Este to invite him to Ferrara in January 1535. Federico Gonzaga gave his consent and the following month Giulio was already able to present a plan for the restoration of the Palazzo Ducale in Ferrara, which had been damaged by fire. Records show that the work was carried out between March 1535 and January 1536.

This was the first of a number of short journeys to satisfy at least some of the requests coming from other cities, including Casale Monferrato in 1536, Ferrara again, in 1537 (but Federico Gonzaga prevented Giulio from going), Bologna and Reggio Emilia in 1538.

Already at the time of his work on the Palazzo Ducale in Ferrara, Giulio's sight was failing, as he frequently complained, and this was to prevent him from working with his usual vivacity. In a letter of 27 April 1539, accompanying a drawing sent to Pietro Aretino, he presents his excuses "for the infirmity of my eyes." Despite this problem, commissions continued to flow in, and it does not seem that Giulio was ever compelled to reject them. In May and June of 1538 he executed the paintings for the Gonzaga's residence at Marmirolo; in 1538-1539 the Padiglione della Rustica was built in the area of the castle at the Ducal Palace; also in 1539 he made drawings for the court of Carlo Bologna at Marengo; and in July 1540 he designed the trappings for the funeral of Federico Gonzaga in the church of Santa Paola. On this occasion Giulio managed in only two weeks to complete the furnishings, a catafalque with alternate columns, and statues and paintings ranged along the nave of the church, transforming the total image of the interior.

The death of Federico Gonzaga, who for fifteen years had been a highly demanding but equally generous patron, monopolizing Giulio's talents, was followed by the assumption of power by Cardinal Ercole Gonzaga, who did not share his predecessor's jealous control over the court artists. This enabled Giulio to extend his field of action and lengthen his visits to other cities.

Between 1540 and 1544 he was responsible for the reconstruction of the abbey church of San Benedetto in Polirone, while he also underwrote a contract with the monastery for the production of six altarpieces.

In 1541 Charles V planned a solemn entrance into the city of Milan, in response to an invitation from the city's governor, the *marchese* del Vasto, and with the purpose of quieting anti-Spanish feeling and resentment over heavy taxation. Because of the success of Giulio Romano's designs for Charles V's entry to Mantua in 1530, the artist was again called on to design the pageantry surrounding this second occasion: it was based on the arms of Charles V and the city of Milan, as a tribute paid by the eight cities and four rivers of the Milanese state to the Emperor, with allusions to Roman heroes and the Empire.

The following year Ercole Gonzaga freely permitted Giulio to meet the requests of Cardinal Francesco Pisani for the decoration of a villa in the Padua area (August) as well as of a commission from Vicenza for the completion of the loggias of the Palazzo della Ragione.

The last four years of Giulio Romano's life are studded with records of the ailments that afflict-

Granada, Palace of Charles V.

14

ed him. In January 1545 there was a false report of his death, as we know from a letter by Pietro Aretino expressing relief at hearing that Giulio was alive and had recovered his health. The last important task he completed was the reconstruction—presumably only of the interiors—of the cathedral of Mantua. Giulio Romano died on 1 November 1546. A few days earlier, according to Vasari, he had been offered the post of architect in the construction of St. Peter's in Rome.

The Legacy

In attempting a critical study of Giulio Romano's achievement, it is indispensable to distinguish the work of the painter from that of the architect. This is not because of any difference in significance, since most of his work consisted in designing buildings and their painted decorations, but because of the differences in the expressive means peculiar to each, and hence of the results, which distinguish the two art forms. The earliest recognition of Giulio's work as an architect was by Sebastiano Serlio in his *Quarto libro* (1527), who stated that the blending of natural elements and the work of man which can be found in various forms of art "... was more pleasing to Giulio Romano than to any other man, as Rome shows in many places and also Mantua, in the beautiful Palazzo del Te... a true example of architecture and painting for our times."

It is precisely this "blending" that is the characteristic feature of Giulio's artistic language, and hence the element that was most widely imitated by his early followers, together with the use of some of this most innovatory ideas, especially those that could be repeated outside their Mantuan framework. Clear examples are the three entrance arches to the Atrio delle Muse in Palazzo Te, which recur in Palazzo Canossa in Verona and the Palazzo Corner in Venice by Sansovino. Giulio Romano's influence on architecture was confined—with few exceptions—to northern Italy, in Emilia and especially in the Po valley. Here the fusion of rustic features and artistic elaboration was combined with a vivacity of expression which took the form of liberation from the austere schemes of the canons of classical art. An echo of these stylistic features can be found in other countries, as in the Arkadenhalle of Neugebäude in Vienna and the loggia in the

Waldstein Palace in Prague. A closer imitation of Giulio's style appears in Charles V's palace in Granada, where the general plan, rustic order, arched loggia and the staggering of the orders are all recognizably in his manner. This is hardly surprising if one remembers that (already in 1527) the ambassador then resident was Baldassarre Castiglione, who probably helped to spread Giulio's ideas.

The critics have stressed five qualities in Giulio Romano's work as a painter: the influence of Raphael; his personal virtuosity and inventiveness; his imperfect execution; his erudition; and his licentiousness. Judgements on each of these points naturally differ, and the same is true of estimates of his standing as a painter. In 1662 Freart, *seigneur* of Chambray, in his *L'idée de la perfection de la peinture*, wrote: "On his death Raphael seems to have bequeathed almost all of his genius to Giulio." But forty years later Piles, in his famous *Bilancia dei pittori*, awarded Giulio sixteen points less than Raphael because of the poor quality of his colouring. Similar doubts about the value of Giulio's work were provoked by his licentiousness, which was at times condemned as mere vulgarity and at others recognized as containing glimmerings of genius.

In the nineteenth century virtuosity and the art of sketching were considered symptoms of decline, and these are the cornerstones of Giulio's art, which often also deals with "lewd" subjects, and this led various authoritative histories of art to condemn it as "no longer in the sphere of Christian art." But the same features also led to its appreciation by other critics. An important historian like Carlo D'Arco stated in 1838: [Giulio] was quick to seize the expression of every other feeling and passion. He makes one see desire, lust, vengeance, suspicion, jealous rage and envy with eminent skill... so that Giulio added a marvellous expressiveness to his paintings through the vehemence of his daring genius."

Today, when our judgements are no longer conditioned by a restrictive morality, critics are agreed in regarding Giulio Romano—a learned master of the classical world, a creative virtuoso and a licentious genius—as one of the founders of a school of painting that is of capital importance in the history of European art—Mannerism.

Anthology of Comments

I lose no opportunity to urge Giulio the painter to come with me to Mantua, and I hope in some way to bring him there, because he has a great desire to do so and only waits until he is satisfied with the painted chamber of the Pope, which has turned out to be very beautiful.
(B. Castiglione, Letter to the *marchese* Federico Gonzaga, 5 September 1524)

I am sorry not to have served your worship sooner and better, excusing myself by the infirmity of my eyes, which only on Easter Sunday allowed me to write to you. And besides my lord the Duke and the illustrious Duchess when setting out left and imposed on me many tasks, so that I was barely able to find an hour's time in which to execute this badly composed drawing; which your worship will think strange news, for no one has ever seen anything by me in pen, and since I have not practised this long enough, I am not skilled in working with it; but as far as I am able to use it, it will always be at your service: and I would say, if it pleases you that for the whole of my life your worship will be provided with such works, offering them with all my strength sincerely applied and not feigned. Nor do I offer them with a view to receiving praise, but merely because it seems to me to be the custom with a friend. And begging you to forgive me if I have been negligent or tardy, I kiss your hands.
(G. Romano, Letter to P. Aretino, 27 April 1539)

If you, illustrious painter and incomparable architect, asked what Titian is doing and what I am awaiting, you would be answered that the thoughts of us two seek no other thing but to find the way to revenge the blow which your promising to come here [to Venice] has given to the affection that our souls feel towards you; for which we are still indignant. He is angry with himself for having shown such vanity to me, and I am angry myself for having believed you. Whence his anger and my irritation will not be dissolved in the fumes they exhale until you keep the promise which you have so often broken. But hope for such a thing is vain, for he that is so cruel in absenting himself from his own home cannot be benevolent in visiting others... And to speak freely to you, for myself, when I remember your manners and your virtues, I would de-

sire not to have either humanity or judgement; for if I lacked them I would not consume myself in the desire to see you work and to be able to take pleasure from it.
(P. Aretino, Letter to G. Romano, June 1542)

[It can be said that Giulio was] probably more graceful than the painting, for he was always happier in expressing his ideas in drawing than in painting, obtaining more vivacity, vigour and expression, possibly because a design is made in an hour in heat, while a painting takes months and years. Thus he became tired, losing his first ardour, and it is no wonder that the paintings are inferior... Giulio built himself a house at Mantua opposite S. Barnaba, with a fantastic façade in coloured stucco, the inside being similarly decorated, and furnished with numerous antiquities brought from Rome and received from the duke, to whom he gave many of his own... At this time Giorgio Vasari, a great friend of Giulio, though they only knew each other by report and by letters, passed through Mantua on his way to Venice to see him and his works. On meeting they recognised each other as though they had met a thousand times before. Giulio was so delighted that he spent four days in showing Vasari all his works, especially the plans of ancient buildings at Rome, Naples, Pozzuolo, Campagna, and all the other principal antiquities designed partly by him and partly others. Then opening a great cupboard, he showed him plans of all the buildings erected from his designs in Mantua, Rome and all Lombardy, so beautiful that I do not believe that more original, fanciful or convenient buildings exist. When the cardinal afterwards asked Giorgio, in Giulio's presence, what he thought of Giulio's work, he answered that he deserved a statue to every corner of the city and half the state would not suffice at reward his labours. The cardinal answered that Giulio was much more the master of the state than himself... He was of medium stature, rather plump than thin, dark skinned, a handsome face, black and laughing eyes, most amiable, of courtly manners, a small eater, and elegant in his dress and bearing.
(G. Vasari, *Le vite de' più eccellenti pittori, scultori e architettori*, Florence 1568. English translation by A.B. Hinds, London 1963)

Let us examine the special merits of Giulio, so as to be able to estimate his precise value in art. And first of all we can speak of inventiveness, the spirit and life of all works of this kind, when they are adapted to the thing one wants to represent, and possess that moderate variety and propriety that it is vain to try to define; this is a merit that was granted to few but was eminent in Giulio. Of a very fertile imagination, even when he was very young he had only to hear an account of an event and at once he would devise the way to depict it, and the fitting poses of the figures who were to play a part in it. This quick imagination was then chastened with lengthy and continuous studies which helped him to seize the essential aspect to be embodied in a drawing, at the same time eliminating whatever was exaggerated or overdone. And in the case of difficult subjects, where the story enabled the poet to range more freely, here too Giulio's talent appeared most clearly. He was truly a painter of lofty conceptions. And this genius, so inclined to magnificence never deceived himself by falling into speciousness seeking for effect which would give momentary pleasure, but directly seeking after the truth and expressing elevated, lasting feelings, he achieved the result that the viewer is always moved. And he well understood how the human mind grasps lofty conceptions and through innovation triumphs and satisfies, for his paintings always contain the marvellous and the great.
(C. D'Arco, *Istoria della vita e delle opere di Giulio Pippi Romano*, Mantua 1838)

During this period of Giulio Romano's unexpected success in Rome, one of the most surprising phenomena is his independence from contemporary movements in Italian painting...This peculiar isolation from contemporary developments is a source at once of weakness and of strength for Giulio. He loses the fraternal association with a great school which can make the work of minor artists often look, by mere suggestion of their associates, better than it really is. He loses also the element of competition which is so sharp a spur to excellence. Toward the end of is career in Mantua in fact, his unchallenged control of the artistic scene even provokes a dangerous carelessness of execution. But in Rome he is still young, and is still able to play subtle personal

variations on High Renaissance themes invented by greater minds. These grand ideas he embroiders, during the elegant, cultivated and spiritually empty reigns of the Medici popes, with his own delightful poetry... Once on his own, Giulio also gives vent to predilection for the garrulous, the fantastic, the rhetorical, which had been held in check while he assisted Raphael and had in certain cases been firmly suppressed. And for the first time he is able to find large-scale expression for the deep inner current of tragedy and terror which is to obsess his latest years. While Raphaelesque types and many aspects of Raphael's spiral figural construction are assimilated into Giulio's independent manner, the style becomes more elegant and elaborate. Polyphonic linear patterns replace the former statuesque solidity.
(F. Hartt, *Giulio Romano*, New Haven 1958)

Giulio lacked roots of his own in the world of the humanists, so that he did not have to experience in his own person the crisis of transformation that afflicted artists like Michelangelo and Pontormo, and as he worked in a period of great productivity and apparent prosperity alongside Raphael, while being also influenced by Michelangelo and perhaps Sebastiano, he was nurtured largely by that special kind of erudite and literary classicism and the passion for rhetoric that was a feature of the court of Leo X, to the point where it even influenced the allocation of ecclesistical benefices, and all this with a relative facility and lightness of spirit.
As has been pointed out, the difficult equilibrium of Raphael's art eluded him, being the fruit of meditated experiences as well as a temperament already inclined towards harmony. The result was that even in the heart of his work in Raphael's circle, in the Stanze Vaticane, we observe a staticity in his figures in formal themes, a transformation of the "action," the quintessence of Renaissance art, into a "gesture," which is a stiffening of form... Giulio's acceptance of the real no longer has the frankness of that of Raphael, because it clashed with opposing inclinations. He also lacked any profound spiritual and religious problems. His classicism, though voluminous, no longer has the subtly critical, ethical and constructive substance of early humanism; it

accepts undiscriminatingly, and takes the form of a rhetorical courtly celebration, and with its heaviness necessarily produces imbalances. Eventually this rhetoric becomes negation, not intellectualized but emotional, almost swelling until it explodes. And it becomes a negation of the classical spirit which grew out of classicism itself, one of the distinctive forms of Mannerism, not so much in painting as in architecture.
(G. Nicco Fasola, "Giulio Romano e il Manierismo," in *Commentari*, 1, IX, 1960)

Giulio Romano is the only direct pupil of Raphael's who with his mannerism developed completely new forms, independent of his master's aims. His use of dark colouring had always produced a slightly alien effect in Raphael's school, but he first found his own special, unorthodox artistic language in the decorations of the Palazzo del Té at Mantua (1532-1534), notably in his *Fall of the Giants*, a fresco that covers the walls of a whole room. Here he strikes a new note, not only in the style of the school, but also in mannerism as a whole. There were already examples of the strange, mysterious, and sinister in the art of Rosso and Beccafumi, but the rendering of a vision as nightmarish as this was a complete innovation in Italian art. The dream was to become a favourite mannerist theme, particularly in literature, and here it assumes the form of an anxiety dream. It should not of course be assumed that fear of life and an atmosphere of impending doom prevailed at the court of a Renaissance prince of the type of Federico Gonzaga, but ten or twenty years earlier it would neither have occurred to any princely connoisseur to have one of his rooms decorated with a horror picture of this kind, nor would he have approved of it. But the very fact that anyone should take pleasure in a picture that creates the impression that the whole room is on the point of collapse and that everything is about to disintegrate into chaos is highly remarkable in such an environment. The taste for horrors, for giants and monsters, for battles of Titans and cataclysms, was, however, far from being a private idiosyncray of Federico Gonzaga's or Giulio Romano's. On the contrary, it was widespread, as is illustrated by the universal popularity of such an unusual subject as the Cyclops Polyphemus. To quote a few

examples only, apart from the use made of it by Giulio Romano in the Palazzo del Té, Sebastiano del Piombo uses it in the Farnesina and Pellegrino Tibaldi in the Palazzo Poggi at Bologna; and Góngora also makes Polyphemus the hero of one of his longer poems.
(A. Hauser, *Il Manierismo*, Turin 1964)

The plan in Giulio's hands is disconcerting and stimulating.
Since he had chosen only this for the commemoration, we can presume that it was more important than usual to him. It is also reasonable to conclude that it was produced for Federico Gonzaga, since Giulio was his court architect. On the whole the spirit of the project is very close to the two designs, made, it seems, for a villa which had a ring of rooms around a central garden, copied from Heemskerck's book of sketches and thought to be Giulio's work. The present project seems to confirm this. But the building is clearly a religious one, and does not seem to be very large. It is more than a chapel but—to judge by the slender walls and a bay formed by the paired columns—it is far from being a cathedral. The design is ingenious... In the absence of a caption or a surviving building, any interpretation of the purpose of this drawing by Giulio is forced to be conjectural. Various hypotheses come to mind, but only one strikes me as probable. I believe it could be the design for the Palatine church in Mantua, which was named Santa Barbara when it was finally built.
(J. Shearman, "Titian's Portrait of Giulio Romano," in *The Burlington Magazine*, CVII, 1965)

Giulio Romano's work in Mantua made good use of his recent experience of the "third manner," in a medium-sized city.
His immediate model was the work of Raphael in Rome, and he followed the same methods. The artist's task was to coordinate the city's artistic activity; he possessed an official title to enable him to do so, a practice that became common in sixteenth and seventeenth century courts. He intervened personally to execute or add a finishing touch to some work of special importance, but he made large use of assistants, and in architectural planning his personal contribution was indistinguishable from that of others. His position in

the cycle of production was like that of a theatrical director, and was made necessary by the crisis in patronage and the increased specialization of his individual collaborators.
Giulio Romano's team of helpers included a large number of specialists: Rinaldo Mantovano, Benedetto Pagni, G.B. Bertani, G.B. Scultori, Niccolò da Milano, Teodoro Ghisi, Francesco Segala, and a number of more eminent figures, such as Francesco Primaticcio, Giovanni da Udine, Polidoro da Caravaggio. In some cases he also worked with highly celebrated artists, as was the case with Titian in 1536, who painted the portraits of the emperors for Duke Federico's Gabinetto dei Cesari.
With the exception of those in Rome, the group of artists brought to Mantua in the first half of the sixteenth century was the most important in Italy, and can be compared to the group working in Urbino fifty years earlier. But no Gonzaga was capable of playing the part played by Federico di Montefeltro; hence the coordination of the various fields of activity passed from the politicians to the artists themselves, and this episode acquired a superstructural character, which was revealed clearly in the sphere of town planning. Giulio Romano's group was capable of decorating a city, not of transforming it.
(L. Benevolo, *Storia dell'architettura del Rinascimento*, Bari 1968)

Giulio was both Federico's architect and also his decorator, his absolute "*régisseur*" of all artistic activity in Mantua.
He brought to his work in Mantua the organization of the workshop which Raphael had devised and he had inherited, but Giulio did not delegate his authority to the executors of his orders. They remained virtually passive figures in the demonstration of his style and the illustration of his ideas.
Giulio's achievements in Mantua, with their originality and richness of ideas, were among the most characteristic and energetic expressions of the Mannerist style... His output was outstanding both in range and quality, but his influences on contemporary art and later art in northern Italy were less important than the work itself.
A fundamental feature of Giulio's art, his assimilation of the Roman energy and sculptural qual-

ities, had, one might say, a regenerating effect on the by now aging Titian, and this was its most important consequence. In addition, certain painters active in the Emilia area adopted aspects of Giulio's art by reflection, but he never had a widespread school. His style—and character—were too extravagant and difficult to digest to have a wide following.
(S.J. Friedberg, "Painting in Italy 1500–1600," in *The Pelican History of Art*, London 1971)

Similar in every way to the typical residence of a citizen of Mantua, the house bought by Giulio in 1538 was thus fairly modest. It was only twenty metres wide and did not include the two bays now on the far right. In depth it did not extend back from the streetfront more than twelve metres and there was no loggia at the rear. The main entrance, situated where the third is now, was linked by a corridor to a narrow staircase at the rear to the left. The façade, which probably comprised two floors and a ceiling had an asymmetrical arrangement. The door was placed off-centre to the left and the windows were set at irregular intervals.
We do not know when Giulio first entered his new house, but reliable evidence suggests that he did not do so at once. It appears that the internal decorations and those on the façade took some years to complete. According to Hartt, probably due to Giulio's heavy work load, the conversion of the house was delayed till after the death of Federico Gonzaga in 1540, but completed before Vasari's visit in 1544. During the restoration of the building in the nineteenth century, the inscription 1544 was found. These facts make it hard to believe that the house which Giulio indicated as his in the letter of 23 April 1539 was the building in Via Poma.
(K.W. Forster, R.J. Tuttle, "The Casa Pippi. Giulio Romano's House in Mantua," in *Architectura*, 1973)

The fact that Raphael was overwhelmed with work in the last year of his life, and delegated much of his pictorial work to his highly organized studio, does not explain the extraordinary blindness of the art historians before the quality of the best of the last paintings, nor their equally surprising overestimate of Giulio Romano. As

we have seen, the reason for this mistaken assessment of Giulio is most likely a questionable theory of pictorial evolution: the idea that mellowness of touch is progress and hence a vigorous touch is a step backwards. But if it were possible to physically superimpose the *Transfiguration* on Giulio's altarpieces in Genoa and Santa Maria dell'Anima, the *Fornarina* on the paintings in Moscow and Strasbourg and *La Perla* on the *Madonna del Gatto*, things would be clear to everyone.
(C. Gould, "Raphael versus Giulio Romano: The Swing Back," in *The Burlington Magazine*, CXXIV, 1982)

The kind of oppressiveness we have felt is completely new and the feeling from which it springs is anguish. In this regard one need only think of the Sala dei Giganti: there we saw at first hand and in a wholly unprecedented way the haunting nightmare of our involvement in an unavoidable catastrophe.
The other element that must not be underrated is the intensity of these terrible and tormenting depictions, which touch upon the pathological. This becomes especially evident if one thinks that the images and fantasies that were permitted to be expressed with all their force through the consent of a prince, as in the Sala dei Giganti, reveal themselves as actually typical of Giulio's work. In fact, if we study them carefully, images of this kind can be found more or less everywhere... But what prevents us from shaking off a particularly morbid impression is not the dramatic paintings in themselves so much as the stereotyped repetition of different scenes which are yet intrinsically homogeneous, which continually recur, only in changing contexts. We keep seeing the same grimaces of bearded old men, repulsive and always menacing, who in their turn are threatened from above or even annihilated.
(E.H. Gombrich, "L'Opera di Giulio Romano," in *Quaderni di Palazzo Te*, 1, I, 1984)

We know little of Giulio's private life in Rome. The rare records, however, insinuate a suspicion of a life that was far from irreprehensible, very different from the "excellent manners" that Vasari credits him with later.

He mixed with the carefree company led by that scapegrace Benvenuto Cellini (another of his companions was Giovan Francesco Penni, likewise a pupil of Raphael, who was to follow Giulio to Mantua). In his autobiography Cellini tells of the Roman nights of the band, in ill-famed taverns, carousing, jesting and mingling with prostitutes.

(P. Carpeggiani, C. Tellini Perina, *Giulio Romano a Mantova "...una nuova e stravagante maniera,"* Mantua 1987)

1

1-3. *Raphael and assistants,* Loggia
di Psiche, *before 1519, the*
Farnesina, Rome.
The Farnesina is a splendid example
of a Renaissance villa, designed and
built between 1508 and 1511 by
Baldassarre Peruzzi for the banker
Agostino Chigi. Because of exposure

to atmospheric agents and also a
number of restoration projects it is
now difficult to identify the hand
of Giulio Romano in the frescoes.
For the same reasons, the figures
of the gods and the atmosphere in
which they were depicted, above all in
the central scene, have lost immediacy

and vividness.
It is quite clear, however, that this
cycle is the forerunner of the frescoes
of the Sala di Amore in the Palazzo
Te (Plates 21, 25), with which it
shares the presentation of human
nudes on a grand scale and sensuous
forms.

4. Giulio Romano, after a drawing by Raphael, The Crossing of the Red Sea, *before 1518. Palazzi Vaticani, Logge, Rome.*

The logge comprise thirteen bays and are decorated with fifty-two episodes, forty-eight from the Old Testament and four from the New. These make up the "Bible of Raphael," to be compared with the "Bible of Michelangelo" which can be admired in the vault of the Sistine Chapel. Set in the eighth bay, the scene shown is part of a cycle (also including the **Deluge** and episodes from the life of Moses) which is homogeneous in style and can be confidently attributed to Giulio Romano, whose contribution to the other frescoes in the logge seems to have been limited to verification of the fidelity of their execution to Raphael's drawings.

4

5

5-7. *Giulio Romano, after a drawing by Raphael,* Constantine Addressing his Army, *before 1522. Palazzi Vaticani, Sala di Costantino, Rome.*

As can be seen in certain drawings, including the above work, as well as in the Battle of Constantine *(Plate 8), Raphael prepared the whole of each scene with his own hand and Giulio kept faithfully to these schemes,* save for some details in the conception of this fresco, in which he accentuates the diagonal line or the running figures in depth, shifting the right-hand group further into the background. In this way the action becomes much less dramatic than in Raphael's scheme, but is enriched with descriptive details, such as the view of Rome and the curtain on the left.

EN TOYTΩI NIKA.

SAVE

MODERATIO

CLEMENS·I

ADLOCVTIO
QVADIVINI

8

8. *Giulio Romano after a drawing
by Raphael, the* Battle of
Constantine, *before 1522. Palazzi
Vaticani, Sala di Costantino, Rome.*

9

9. *Giulio Romano and Raphael (?),*
Portrait of Joanna of Aragon,
1518. Louvre, Paris.
Joanna of Aragon, the niece of
Ferdinand I, King of Aragon, was
considered such a perfect example of
beauty that a treatise was actually
devoted to her. In his Lives of the
Painters *Vasari states that Raphael*
"only made... a life-size portrait of the
head, and the rest was done by
Giulio." The accentuated
characterization of the figure and the
lack of three-dimensional qualities
make it unlikely that Raphael painted
the whole portrait. Recent studies also
suggest that his share of the work was
confined to the face.

10. *Giulio Romano and*
Gianfrancesco Penni, Coronation
of the Virgin of Monteluce,
c. 1523. Pinacoteca Vaticana, Rome.

11

11, 12. Christ in Glory with Four Saints (Deesis), *c. 1520-1524.* Pinacoteca Nazionale, Parma. *Owing to affinities with a drawing by Raphael now in the Paul Getty Museum in Malibu, it is likely that the painting was originally commissioned from Raphael and that Giulio executed it after his death from preparatory sketches. As compared with the Christ of Raphael that of Giulio Romano has a more static and frontal pose which is clearly meant to be more hieratic, while the figures are closer in the foreground and face the viewer. The exceptional quality of the colouring around the figure of Jesus and the gloomy light below deliberately stress the glory of the divine manifestation.*

13

13, 14. Sacra Conversazione, *c. 1522-1523. Santa Maria dell'Anima, Rome.* *This is almost certainly the first altarpiece wholly devised by Giulio, who seems not to have used any* drawings by Raphael. This is confirmed by the fact that the scene is not arranged symmetrically and the difference between the divine and the human is stressed by the rhetorical gestures of the saints before the sudden apparition, in contrast with the image of the old woman in the background, intent on feeding the chickens. The visionary atmosphere offers a synthesis of the experience of Giulio and his love for classical antiquity.

15

15. Virgin and Child, *1520-1522.*
Galleria degli Uffizi, Florence.
The execution clearly reflects the
references to previous work by
Raphael, above all in the features of
the Virgin, very similar to those of the
Fornarina, *of which it repeats the*
form of the nose, here slightly less
fleshy, and the lips.

16

16. Hertz Madonna, *c. 1521-1522.*
Palazzo Barberini Rome.
The painting, with its domestic
setting— a bedroom with a perspective
view opening into a corridor—was
intended for private devotion.

Certain elements, such as the detailed
depiction of objects and the use of
light, suggest an interest in Flemish
art, while the frontal arrangement
recalls the Florentine drawings of
Raphael.

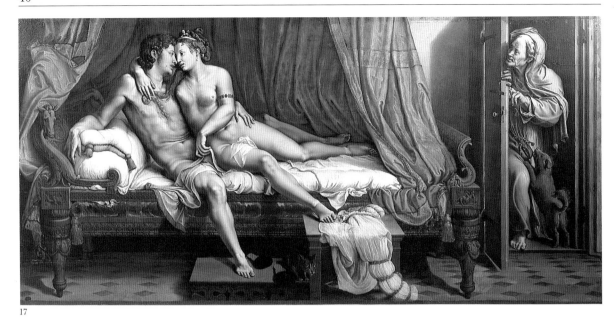

17

17, 18. Two Lovers, *1524-1525.*
Hermitage, Leningrad.
This painting can be conjecturally
dated to the period immediately
following Giulio's arrival in Mantua,
as a work in the erotic genre that had
enjoyed so much success in Rome. The
arrangement of the scene is
comparable to the drawings of the
Modi. *In its dimensions (more than*
three metres wide) and technical
virtuosity there is nothing like this in
the whole of Italian Renaissance
painting. The title with which it is
exhibited at the Hermitage,
Alexander and Ariadne, *is*
certainly not the original one, as the
theme does not belong to mythology or
ancient history, but is instead typical
of the circle of Pietro Aretino.

19

19, 20. Sala dei Cavalli, *c. 1526.*
Palazzo Te, Mantua.
The plan for this stateroom, the largest
in the Palazzo Te, was one of Giulio's
first designs in Mantua. The
decoration was conceived with
constant reference to the figure of

Federico Gonzaga and his public and
private roles, with divinities serving as
symbols of the virtues and sentiments.
The motto contained in the emblem of
the salamander is significant in this
regard: "Quod huic deest me
torquet" *("that which this creature*

lacks is a torment to me"), a clear
allusion to amorous matters.
While the work was mainly executed
by pupils, Giulio was certainly
responsible for Hercules and
Deianira, *above the horse* Glorioso,
and many other equestrian figures.

44

21, 22. Giulio Romano and assistants, The Noble Banquet, *c. 1526-1528. Sala di Amore, Palazzo Te, Mantua.*
The Sala di Amore presents the most imposing decorative scheme in the entire palace, save for the Sala dei Giganti. The decoration is divided into three parts: on the ceiling and the south wall there are episodes from the fable by Apuleius, culminating in the central panel in the ceiling with the Marriage of Cupid and Psyche *(Plate 23). The south and west walls illustrate the nuptial banquet, with respectively the* Noble Banquet *(Plates 21, 22) and the* Rustic Banquet, *while the north wall has mythological scenes as well as good and bad examples of love, such as* Acis and Galatea, Zeus and Olympiades, Pasiphaë and the Bull. *The whole chamber is testimony to Giulio's stylistic development in his early period in Mantua, starting from the ceiling, where there are evident signs of the still close relationship with his works in Rome.*

23

23. Giulio Romano and assistants,
The Marriage of Cupid and
Psyche, *c. 1526-1528. Sala di
Amore, Palazzo Te, Mantua.*

24

24. *Giulio Romano and assistants,*
The Ordeal of the Choice of the
Seeds, *c. 1526-1528. Sala di Amore,*
Palazzo Te, Mantua.

25. *Giulio Romano and assistants,*
Mars and Venus at the Bath,
detail, c. 1526-1528. Sala di Amore,
Palazzo Te, Mantua.

50

26-31. *Giulio Romano and assistants,*
Sala dei Giganti, *c. 1526-1534.*
Palazzo Te, Mantua.
The walls of this chamber are almost
wholly the work of Rinaldo da Faenza
and he is responsible for the two-
dimensional effect of the whole and
the impression of outstanding
coherence. The vaulting, however,
raises problems of attribution: Giulio's
hand is evident mainly in the
principal group of Jove and Juno and
in the scenes framing Diana, while the
rest was the work of assistants, though
a precise division of their work is not
possible. In this room Giulio's great
merit was to supervise the work of his
pupils to create an extremely
homogeneous whole.

32

32, 33. Giulio Romano and assistants, Sala di Troia, c. 1536-1540. Palazzo Ducale, Mantua. No records exist to help identify the artists responsible for the various scenes, but the enormous amount

of work involved suggests that Giulio would have only provided some of the finishing touches. The decoration illustrates scenes of warfare and other episodes which led to the fall of Troy. Numerous

divinities control the outcome of events so that everything happens as predestined. The chamber is decorated in such a way that it makes a strong emotional impact upon the viewer, who is almost overwhelmed by the

power of the paintings.
The scenes allude to the political
successes of Federico Gonzaga in the
1530s, while the exaltation of the
Greek heroes is a tribute to the
Paleologa family.

33

Essential Bibliography

C. D'Arco, *Istoria della vita e delle opere di Giulio Pippi Romano* (Mantua 1838) 2nd ed. 1842.

G. Paccagnini, *Il Palazzo Te*, Milan 1957.

F. Hartt, *Giulio Romano*, New Haven 1958.

Studi su Giulio Romano, San Benedetto Po 1975.

G. Vasari, *Le vite de' più eccellenti pittori, scultori e architettori.* (Florence 1568)³ Milan 1929, replica edition, Florence 1981. (English ed., *The Lives of the Painters, Sculptors and Architects*, trans. by A.B. Hinds, J.M. Dent Sons Ltd., London 1963).

D. Arasse, "Giulio Romano e il labirinto di Psiche," in *Quaderni di Palazzo Te*, 3, II, 1985, pp. 7-18.

P. Carpeggiani, C. Tellini Perina, *Giulio Romano a Mantova "... una nuova e stravagante maniera,"* Mantua 1987.

G.M. Erbesato, *Il Palazzo Te di Giulio Romano*, Florence 1987.

A. Belluzzi, "Giulio di Raffaello da Urbino," in *Quaderni di Palazzo Te*, 8 IV, 1988, pp. 9-20.

Giulio Romano, exhibition catalogue, Mantua, Palazzo Te and Palazzo Ducale, Milan 1989.

G. Suitner, C. Tellini Perina, *Palazzo Te, Mantova*, Milan 1990.

Photographic Credits
Sergio Anelli, Milan
Elemond Archives, Milan
Giancarlo Giovetti, Mantua
Nimatalah/Luisa Ricciarini, Milan
Marco Ravenna, Correggio (Re)
Scala, Florence

Printed for Arnoldo Mondadori Arte
by Fantonigrafica - Elemond Editori Associati